MW01075713

RENEWING YOUR MIND

A Mindset Book For Spiritual Warfare And
Victorious Living

(Spiritual Warfare Series)

By Lynn R Davis

PUBLISHED BY: Lynn R Davis

Be the first to know when my books are free.
Visit: LynnRDavis.com today to register your
email address.

Most Popular Titles by Lynn

Deliver Me From Negative
Self Talk A Guide To Speaking
Faith-filled Words

How God Sees Your Struggles: Encouraging Yourself,
Finding Strength & Developing a Spiritual Perspective

Deliver Me from Negative Emotions: Controlling
Emotions and Finding Peace in the Storm

CONTENTS

Introduction

INTRODUCTION

"Behold, his soul which is lifted up is not upright in him: but the just shall live by his faith." (Habakkuk 2:4)

Ever feel like your faith is failing or not working? I can relate.

From the age of three until age 18, I spent practically every day in church. But, when I left home for college, even with all of that churching, it still took a while for me to understand the significant difference between living by faith and living by *going to church*.

I was going through the religious motions, but my mind wasn't renewed. To live by faith we must possess a particular *mindset*. I will refer this frame of mind as the *faith mindset*. This state of mind not only **believes** all things are possible through Christ, it **knows** it without a doubt.

Living by faith goes beyond your daily religious activities and church affiliations. There has to be a mind *and* body spiritual connection.

It's easy to get so wrapped up in the physical activity that we neglect the mental piece, but a faith mindset is the glue that will keep you from falling apart in a spiritual battle.

We can't just memorize scripture, we have to believe it. We can't just go to church, we have to be the church. Being requires believing and that means you have to adopt the mind of Christ.

Even after I'd spent hours in church, I still hated my life. I was still stressed and depressed to the point of tears.

See, I'd lifted my hands in worship. I'd taken notes during the sermon, but I had not changed my mind about what I was going through. I was bitter, blaming, and resentful. In my mind, I had every right to be all those things and more. My marriage had ended. My mom had just died and in my mind life sucked.

I was a victim of life. I'd gotten a raw deal. That was my mentality. My praise came from the perspective of a victim. My prayers were from the perspective of a victim.

I'm here to tell you, if you are still thinking from the perspective of a victim and have not yet adopted a faith mindset about what you are facing, **you are not** living by faith. You are instead living by fear.

Fear today produces more fear tomorrow. Worry today produces a harvest of more worry in the future. Feeling like a victim today, sets you up for a harvest of being victimized down the line.

You know the saying, you can lead a horse to water but you can't make him drink? Well, all the books and sermons in the world were leading me to faithful living, but because I didn't deliberately change my thinking, I was just standing there, staring at healing waters, choosing to be powerless.

What if the blind man had just sat down in front of the pool of Siloam and never washed the clay from his eyes as Jesus instructed? He'd still be blind. Jesus directed him toward his breakthrough, but it was up to him to do the rest. He had to do his part. He had to have a faith mindset.

Many of us are still blind in the area of faith because we've only done part of what the Word instructs. We're consistently angry, frustrated, and doubtful. We are going to church, serving in groups, but we haven't developed our minds or changed our thinking. Then we wonder why we still feel blind in certain areas of our lives.

God has placed men, women, and ministries in our lives to help direct us, but that's all they can do. The rest is up to us. We have to take the steps to be transformed by the renewing of our minds. We have to develop and practice a faith mindset.

Thankfully, after years of grace, mercy, and spiritual growth, I've grown spiritually and developed a faithful mindset. I still have problems arise, but they don't overtake me. I learned to do my part. It wasn't enough to hear the Word. I had to become a doer also.

"But be ye doers of the word, and not hearers only, deceiving your own selves. But be ye doers of the word" (James 1:22)

I am writing this in hopes that it will strengthen you. Perhaps something in this brief book will strike a chord with you and change your faith life forever.

"But I have prayed for thee, that thy faith fail not: and when thou art converted, strengthen thy brethren. (Luke 22:32)

I don't want your faith to fail. Faith works. It really does. People can doubt it, deny it; try to dispute it, but I'm too far gone to believe otherwise. Too many Scratch-my-head and throw-up-my-hands circumstances have been worked out in my life and the lives of those I love for me to have any doubts about the power of faith and its ability to move mountains.

My Assumptions

As I write, I am assuming: (1) you are a saved Spirit-filled believer. (2) You believe in the power of faith and prayer (3) you believe God has given you the power to be victorious and (4) your heart's desire is to be a spiritual warrior.

I don't want to take number 1 for granted though. Romans 10:9-10 says, "[9] because, if you confess with your mouth that Jesus is Lord and believe in your heart that God raised him from the dead, you will be saved. [10] For with the heart one believes and is justified, and with the mouth one confesses and is saved."

If you are reading this and you desire to live by faith, take this opportunity to accept Christ as your Lord and Savior. Say this prayer:

Dear Lord, I repent for my sins. I ask you to forgive me. I believe that you are the son of God and you died on the cross to save me. I ask you to take control of my life. Come into my heart. I receive you now and make you Lord over my life. Amen.

All of heaven is rejoicing at this very moment (Luke 15:7). If you don't do anything else with this book, it has served its purpose in your life. You have received the gift of salvation by grace through faith. Welcome to the family!

(2) If you want to believe in the power of faith and prayer read on. Prayer works. Faith works. I'm a living witness.

(3) Now that you are part of the family, you have spiritual weapons available to you. You need them because your enemy is not physical. Sure he works through people, but there is a spiritual wickedness in high places (Ephesians 6:12) that you now have the authority, by Christ Jesus, to pull down.

With those assumptions in mind, not everyone is the same. Your modality of faith may be different from mine and that's okay. God is not static, stagnant, or rigid. He is living in, loving and forgiving us all at every stage our spiritual walk.

The Faith Strategy

We all received a measure of faith (Romans 12:3) at the time of salvation. Whether you feel like it or not, you have enough. Faith mixed with action and endurance can overcome anything.

I'm going to share a personal faith "system" with you. The steps I take in a faith fight. I've never been led to share this message before.

This topic has been on my mind for almost a year. I'm only now sharing it because it won't go away. Usually, when a message persists, that means it's for more than just me and I have to write about it.

Someone reading this has been praying for answers. Somewhere in this book, God will give them to you. I pray those drawn to these pages will receive their breakthrough in faith.

I've narrowed the *Faith Strategy* steps/stages to the following:

1. Quarantine The Issue
2. Go Before The Throne of Grace
3. Assemble The Tribe
4. Suspend Your Doubts
5. Make Peace With The Outcome
6. Demonstrate Your Faith
7. Wait and Know
8. Rehearse Your Celebration

Whoever you are, I want you to know that God loves you so much that He inspired these pages and led you to them. Open your heart and mind. You will find the answers you seek.

The Faith Mindset Defined

I took a moment to look at these various definitions for Mind-set and Faith to help better explain my perspective of a Faith Mindset.

Definition-Mind-set: (1) a mental attitude (2) a fixed state of mind.

Definition-Faith: (1) complete trust or confidence

Synonyms: trust, belief, confidence, conviction, optimism, hopefulness, hope

Based on the definitions above and inspiration of the Holy Spirit, my definition of a *Faith Mindset is*: *A mental attitude of complete confidence and trust that the power of God that dwells within and without, will always prevail, and produce a harvest of victory, especially in cases where physical evidence of said victory is non-existent.*

Isn't that powerful? Aren't you ready to live a life a spiritual life void of doubt, fear, anxiety and stress? You can. All you have to do is get rid of the negative BS.

It's Time to Change Your BS (Belief System)

You are where you are because of your B.S. –your belief system. The way you've thought over a long period of time contributed to decisions that led to this very moment. Your BS is the reason you chose certain friends; your mate; your career; etc. All decisions can be traced back to your BS.

Earlier, I described a faith mind-set is as a state of mind that knows all things are possible through Christ Jesus. This sounds good, but let's talk more about the characteristics of a faithful mind so that we have a clearer picture.

1. *A faith mind-set is unmovable and stands firm on the Word.*

1 Corinthians 15:58, "Therefore, my dear brothers and sisters, stand firm. Let nothing move you. Always give yourselves fully to the work of the Lord, because you know that your labor in the Lord is not in vain."

Colossians 3:2, set your mind on things above and keep it set!

2. A faith mind-set believes in the unseen.

Hebrews 11:1, "Now faith is the substance of things hoped for, the evidence of things not seen."

3. A faith mind-set is sober.

Be sober, be vigilant; because your adversary the devil, as a roaring lion, walketh about, seeking whom he may devour: (1 Peter 5:8)

4. A faith mind-set is sound.

Second Timothy 1:7 says, "For God did not give us a spirit of fear, but of power and of love and of a sound mind!"

5. A faith mind-set knows God-inspired labor is never in vain.
    Therefore, my beloved brethren, be ye steadfast, unmovable, always abounding in the work of the Lord, for ye know that your labor is not in vain in the Lord. (1 Corinthians 15:58)

You have to replace your negative BS with a faith-mindset. To do that you must continually saturate your heart and mind with the Word. You surround yourself with faith-minded people. You unfriend negative drama kings and queens. You operate from a faith mindset on purpose until it become automatic. You decide from this day forward, *No more negative BS.*

From Faith-Mind to Faith-Mode

When you have a *Faith Mindset*, and a problem occurs, you automatically go into *Faith-Mode.* You on purpose take actions consistent with biblical principles.

In the beginning it may be a challenge because you're fighting against your "normal" or your pre-programmed response. The good news about programmed responses is that you can change them.

You don't have to yell and scream every time you get angry. That's a preprogrammed response. You can change that with prayer and practice. You can live by faith, but it will take prayer and daily application.

I promise to share this information in the only way I know how: simple, down-to-earth, relatable, and to-the-point. I asked God a long time ago if I should try to write longer more in depth books and immediately I heard, "write the vision and make it plain." So now, unapologetically, that is what I do -K.I.S.S- Keep it simple and spirit-led.

Chapter 1

Quarantine the Issue

"Protect your spirit from contamination. Limit your time with negative people."- Thema Davis

I'm reminded of a scene from the 1982 science fiction movie, E.T, directed by Steven Spielberg. In the scene, scientist enclosed the family's home in an air-tight plastic tent.

Now imagine placing your problem in a similar contained environment- a faith chamber. Inside is everything you need to treat your issue. Your goal is to isolate it from the negative influences of the carnal world.

This first step is vitally important. Something has threatened your spiritual peace and wellbeing. It's a spiritual emergency and quarantining it will help:

1. Protect you from unwanted spectators.
2. Evaluate the different aspects.
3. Avoid jumping to conclusions and acting too hastily.
4. Put you in a faith frame of mind.

For example, suppose you get a negative medical report. What you do is mentally quarantine the bad news:

1. Ask God for strength right then and there.
2. Don't share it, post it, blog it or chat about it.
3. Avoid reading negative research on the internet.
4. Take the negative thoughts captive.

Now that your problem is in this quarantine bubble, imagine it is now surrounded by a shield of faith and the goal is not to let anything contrary to God's will inside that bubble. Let's take a look inside at the spiritual warfare weapons at your disposal:

- Prayer & Meditation
- Your Bible
- Positive Self Talk
- Faith Confessions
- Lovely Thoughts
- Seeds
- Testimonies of Past Victories

Any time you have a prayerful desire or a problem that you know requires God's intervention to achieve, consider quarantining it until you get a handle on exactly what you are dealing with and who you should allow to be a part of the solution.

Don't broadcast it. Take it to God in prayer first. Then people you trust who are solution oriented, not spectators who will reinforce a negative mentality.

We certainly want people who will tell us like it is, but only those who can do so in faith and love. Those people, we will discuss later, will become your Spiritual Tribe.

Prayer and Meditation

Carve out private time with the Father. Communication with God is going to be your lifeline during this process. If you aren't talking to Him more than anyone else, you're setting yourself up for failure. He has all the answers. Ask Him first. Then allow Him to answer however He chooses and that may be through another person or an inspired idea. Stay prayerfully focused on the solution.

Years ago when I was praying for my teenage son's deliverance, I lay away all hours imagining all sorts of terrible things- including planning his funeral. I felt helpless so I worried day and night about where he was; who he was with; and what he was doing.

All of that helplessness and worry was a form of negative meditation. Joshua 1:8 says meditating on the word day and night brings prosperity and success. So it stands to reason, in my mind, that worrying (negative meditation) on my problems day and night will bring lack and failure.

What you meditate on day and night will produce your reality. Every minute of the day you are performing faithful meditation or toxic meditation. That's why it's important not to spend so much time focused on what's going wrong. Choose a peaceful disposition and meditate on a favorable outcome instead.

Keep Your Bible Close

Inspiration for peaceful encouragement comes from the word. Keep your bible near. I don't mean to say you have to carry a five pound bible with you everywhere. I have a downloaded Bible application on my smart phone. I've also signed up for various daily scripture notifications. I have a bible in my car and by my nightstand.

I've gotten lots of inspiration in the middle of the late hours of night or early morning it's a lot easier to turn over and open my bible than it is to get out of bed and find it. Inspirational music; videos; podcasts; and the like are also wonderful sources of spiritual food for your soul.

Many times I've read daily scriptures from devotionals and found just the word that I needed to raise my spirits and maintain a *faith mindset*.

Positive Self Talk and Faith Confessions

Two books later on the subject of eliminating Negative Self Talk, I'm still learning and growing. The negative chatter doesn't just stop. You have to stop it. You have to put up blocks to it that stop it in its tracks. You have to know the difference between the lies and the truth.

Even if the negative chatter has some elements of truth in it. For example, it was absolutely true that I was ten months behind on my mortgage. It was absolutely true that I didn't have $15,000 to pay it. It was true that my credit was shot and I couldn't even borrow the money.

make your focus about

All those thoughts chimed in my head constantly to remind me what I was facing, but the *faith mindset* doesn't practice these thoughts. The faith mindset takes these thoughts captive and casts them down. The *faith mindset* says, "I know all of this is true for now, but my God is well able to deliver me. And even if He chooses not to, I will still serve Him. I know all things will work together for my good!"

This is how the word that you meditate on can become positive self-talk and faith confessions.

Lovely Thoughts

"He will keep in perfect peace all those who trust in Him, whose thoughts turn often to the Lord! Trust in the Lord always, for in the Lord, Jehovah, is your everlasting strength." (Isaiah 26:3-4)

Longtime readers know that I mention Philippians 4:8 in practically all of my books. It's such vital scripture for believers who want to grow in faith. You must win the battle in your mind, before you can manifest victory in the flesh.

"Finally,5 brethren, whatsoever things are true, whatsoever things *are* honest, whatsoever things are just, whatsoever things *are* pure, whatsoever things *are* lovely, whatsoever things *are* of good report; if *there be* any virtue, and if *there be* any praise, think on these things."

Positive Testimonies

The enemy is not coming up with new attack strategies because the old tried and true ones are working very well still to this day. The same things he did to Job, he's using them on many of us. He attacks relationships, resources, and health again and again. He uses the emotion of fear to paralyze our minds and make us believe that we are destined for doom. He's familiar with our BS and he will use it against us as long as we'll allow. Renewing your mind is the only way to clear up your BS and take away the enemy's power.

"So I take pleasure in weaknesses, insults, catastrophes, persecutions, and in pressures, because of Christ. For when I am weak, then I am strong." (Philippians 1:12)

Read and meditate on Ephesians 6:10-18:

[10] Finally, be strong in the Lord and in his mighty power. [11] Put on the full armor of God, so that you can take your stand against the devil's schemes. [12] For our struggle is not against flesh and blood, but against the rulers, against the authorities, against the powers of this dark world and against the spiritual forces of evil in the heavenly realms.

[13] Therefore put on the full armor of God, so that when the day of evil comes, you may be able to stand your ground, and after you have done everything, to stand. [14] Stand firm then, with the belt of truth buckled around your waist, with the breastplate of righteousness in place, [15] and with your feet fitted with the readiness that comes from the gospel of peace.

[16] In addition to all this, take up the shield of faith, with which you can extinguish all the flaming arrows of the evil one. [17] Take the helmet of salvation and the sword of the Spirit, which is the word of God.

[18] And pray in the Spirit on all occasions with all kinds of prayers and requests. With this in mind, be alert and always keep on praying for all the Lord's people.

A FAITH MINDSET BELIEVES:

1. I am resting in the promises of God. This will work out for my good.
2. I don't like this experience but I WILL learn and grow from it.
3. This cannot last forever. Whatever the outcome, I will keep the faith.
4. Even though I'm still a little afraid, I'm not hopeless, and I won't give up.

Chapter 2

Go Before the Throne

(STEP 1)

Lay it all out on the altar. You are going to pray what's called a *prayer of petition* or *prayer of faith*. In this prayer you're asking God for a desired outcome. You're not telling Him what to do, but you're asking Him for what you believe is the best outcome.

Our first step should always be prayer. At times things are happening really quickly and it may seem you have no time to pray. In those instances, consider a short prayer like, "Lord help me." But, for the purposes of this book, I am talking about a more in depth prayer. One in which you will take time to talk with God on a deeper level.

Tell God how you feel. Be honest with God. If you're scared, say that. If you're angry with Him, say that. If you feel embarrassed, tell him that too. Be open about how you really feel. Don't try to suppress anything in the name of being spiritual. Release the fear, anger, hurt, pain from your heart by pouring it all out.

When my grandmother died in a tragic house fire, I had zero understanding of how something like that could happen to such a loving and beautiful woman. I told God I was angry. Why didn't He protect her? Why did she have to die? Didn't He know that I needed her? I blamed people who had driven by and seen the smoke, but didn't stop or call the fire department. I was hurting and I told God who, what, when, where, and why. Tell Him how you feel. He can take it. He is God.

Take the time to thank God for His love, the very love that has delivered you in the past and will deliver you again, because He is the same yesterday, today, and forevermore. At first you may not feel victorious.

You feel like a victim. You're nauseous. You feel like someone has knocked the wind out of you. You're caught off guard and you have no idea what to do next. And you know what? It's okay to feel that way right now. It's just an indication that you have a little spiritually work to do.

Normal fear responses are *fight, flight, or freeze*. Fear makes since in some instances. If I see a snake, God forbid, I'm going to feel fear. That's normal for me. Some people have them for pets. I hate them. They creep me out and in Texas you can run into these reptiles practically anywhere. My fear response says, "Whoa something is threatening your safety and you need act now to stay safe. You're brain has kicked into survival mode and adrenalin is rushing through your body.

In life, when we go through difficult situations, the fear response kicks in. Something is not right and you need to take action. Now, I have no intentions of facing any snakes (shiver) but, in the case of a spiritual battle, you have to face the fear. It's there. It's real. Suppressing it will not get rid of it. It will only show up again in a different way. Fear is based on something you believe-a deep rooted belief caused by some negative or even traumatic experience.

That traumatic experience will remain deeply rooted until you pluck it up through prayer. If you don't, it will bloom doubt, insecurity, and anxiety time and time again.

You have to get to the root in order to change the negative belief. You have to deal with it. How? Face it in prayer. Here is an example of a prayer that I might pray. It's general, but will give you the gist:

God I'm scared. Help me overcome this fear. I know you have not given me a spirit of fear, so I release it to you. Show me your truth about what I am afraid of. Give me wisdom to understand why I am afraid and how I can see this in a more positive light. Your word says you have given me the power to tread on serpents, scorpions, and all manner of evil in the earth. I desire to let that power reign in me. Thank you Father that the light of your love casts out the darkness of my fear. In Jesus name, Amen.

Prayer will give you the power to break down fear. Whether you freeze, fight or flight, God is ready and waiting to cast out fear and fill you with love, "The righteous cry out, and the LORD hears them; he delivers them from all their troubles. The LORD is close to the brokenhearted and saves those who are crushed in spirit." (Psalm 34:17)

Pour out your heart in detail about the problem and how you feel about what's happening. You'll feel better releasing it from your soul. It's okay to cry or pound the pillow. Suppressing anger and pain will come back to bite you in the form of fear and doubt down the line. Let it out now. The Holy Spirit is your comforter and guide. He will comfort you. Ask for healing, strength to be renewed and receive that healing by faith.

You're hurting and all of that negative energy needs an outlet. This is a healthy outlet. It's much better to let it out in prayer than lose it in public or act out of vengeance. Go ahead and pray and cry until the tears slow down or stop. You may even want to journal about your feelings during this process. That's what I did in 2011 during a financial hardship.

End your prayer with praise. Give praise for who He is as the creator of this incredible universe and all that is in it. He's powerful and He loved us enough to place that power within us. Be thankful for that power flowing through you. Acknowledge the blessings and birthrights you have through Jesus Christ. You have a right to healing, victory, abundance, peace, joy and every good and heavenly gift. All of which is available to you now. Praise Him for that. He will inhabit your praise and you will feel His presence.

Sit in the acknowledgement of God's goodness for a time. Reflect on the last time God delivered you. Remember how you felt at the beginning of that circumstance and let yourself feel good knowing that He will deliver you again. It's a matter of you standing in faith; seeing it through His eyes and focusing on the promise, not the problem.

Again, this is what I do. Your prayers may be different. The main thing message is give it to God in prayer. Go boldly before God and lay it all out. Release it. Don't stay in fear and sadness. Let God shift you from fear to faith. When you get up from prayer, you will feel better. You may not know yet what to do, but you do know that you are not doing it alone.

I end my faith prayer by making peace with what is happening and what the outcome may be, not that I'm expecting to be defeated, but I now have a *faith mindset* which means:

- *I am resting in the promises of God that this will work out for my good.*

- *I don't like this experience but I'm going to learn and grow from it.*
- *This cannot last forever and whatever the outcome, I will still trust God.*
- *Even though I'm still a little afraid, I'm not hopeless, and I won't give up.*

These types of prayers require privacy and time. If your schedule is hectic, I understand, but you have to make time to have this discussion with the Father. Prayer warrior prayers that are effectual and fervent take time to pray. They make time. "Therefore confess your sins to each other and pray for each other so that you may be healed. The prayer of a righteous person is powerful and effective." (James 5:16)

In the following days and weeks, I continue to pray to God. I don't pray the exact same prayer though. I've already asked Him for my desired outcome, so my prayer changes to a prayer of thanksgiving. From this moment forward, **I thank God EVERY day that my prayers have been heard and I have what I asked for or something better.**

The following is a brief outline of what that prayer might look like for me.

1. Thank God for His goodness and love now and forever. "Enter into his gates with

thanksgiving, *and* into his courts with praise: be thankful unto him, *and* bless his name." (Psalm 100:4)

2. Forgive everyone involved. Ask forgiveness for yourself and receive it by faith. "And when ye stand praying, forgive, if ye have fought against any: that your Father also which is in heaven may forgive you your trespasses." (Mark 11:25)

3. Acknowledge remaining fears and ask God to help you overcome them. Let us therefore come boldly unto the throne of grace that we may obtain mercy, and find grace to help in time of need. (Hebrews 4:16)

4. Ask God for a new perspective to see it through His eyes. "There is a way which seemeth right unto a man, but the end thereof *are* the ways of death. (Proverbs 14:12)

5. Listen for Answers. Sit still and quiet.

6. Yield to His direction. "For as many as are led by the Spirit of God, they are the sons of God. (Romans 8:14)

7. Thank God that He has already given you what you've asked for or something better. "Ye have not chosen me, but I have chosen you, and ordained you, that ye should go and bring forth fruit, and [that] your fruit should remain: that whatsoever ye shall ask of the

Father in my name, he may give it you." (John 15:16)

*You may not know the **outcome** but know this-you will come out.* Amen. Once I've quarantined the issue and poured my heart and soul onto the altar, and listened for God's voice, I move on to the next step. I notify my tribe.

PRAY FRUITFUL PRAYERS

1. Thank God for His Love That Will Inevitably Deliver
2. Acknowledge Fears and Doubts-Release Them To God
3. Thank God for The Best Outcome For All Involved
4. Reflect on Past Victories. Feel Good About The Outcome
5. Rest in His Peace. Expect Victory No Matter What

Chapter 3

Assemble the Tribe

(STEP 2)

"For by wise guidance you will wage war, and in abundance of counselors there is victory." (Proverbs 24:6)

Call in the troops. Now is the time to contact your "need to know people". Your tribe may consist of those people closest to you or those who you know are Godly, loyal, and care about your well-being.

For some, the tribe will be close friends. For others the council will consist of a mixture of ministers, friends and or family. Most recently, my tribe consisted of my siblings. Sometimes it consists of longtime friends. Tribes do change depending on what the issue is and who you feel led to confide in.

The purpose of your tribe is to offer wise counsel and advice. These are not "yes men". They are the ones who will:

- Mirror God's love and support for you.
- Tell you the honest objective truth about your circumstances.
- Listen to your problem and offer their sincere encouragement.

- Pray with you and agree with you for a victorious outcome.
- Offer assistance where they can.
- Continue to intercede long after the conversation is over.
- Make themselves available to you for support.

Tribal meetings are not for venting, complaining, blaming, and condemning. When you're in a faith fight, you want to avoid all of the negativity. Remember whatever you agree on is what you will have, so if you're sitting around agreeing about how terrible your life is, you will have more of that.

"The way of a fool is right in his own eyes, but a wise man is he who listens to counsel." (Proverbs 12:15)

Wise people will speak wisdom into your life. They will pray with you and help you remain accountable. If you don't feel comfortable consulting others, that's okay too.

I Don't Have (or Want) To Assemble A Tribe

There have been times in my life when my tribe consisted of God, Jesus, and the Holy Spirit. Times when I didn't feel like I could talk to anyone else for fear of being misunderstood or judged. Most of us have experienced such times when the fear, guilt, and or shame keeps us from reaching out to anyone.

A tribe is not something that you take likely or assemble out of desperation. Ask for discernment. Avoid pretenders at all cost. People who appear trustworthy, but lack the integrity necessary to be a confidant. Don't feel like you have to pull a group of people into your situation if that makes you uncomfortable. Take the time to get to know the hearts and minds of the people around you. That usually happens long before you enter a crisis. Relationships take time to build.

Again, use discernment. They don't have to be perfect. None is perfect but the Father. But if a person is willing to help you stir up confusion, they are not a good example of "wise counsel" and you may want to think twice about allowing them in your tribal family.

If you don't have a tribe, consider keeping a prayer journal. In it, share your true day to day feelings with the Lord. Pour out your emotions on to paper. End each entry with prayer and thanksgiving. I kept one during my 21 Day Daniel Fast.

Research has shown that writing is therapeutic and has proven to decrease stress and improve mental health. I mentioned before, several years ago, after an extreme dip in my income, I nearly lost my home. I was ten months behind on my mortgage and stressed beyond belief. I went into *faith mode*. I kept a journal that I actually shared in my book, *How a Hope Seed Grows.*

What do you journal about? When you don't have a tribe, journal about:

- How your day went
- Events that happen big or small
- Outcomes you desire
- Brainstorms of possible solutions
- Prayers and faith confessions
- Scriptures that encourage you
- Faith confessions and prayers

The possibilities are endless. You will find that God begins to speak to you through your journaling experience. Your answer could be just a journal entry away. You don't have to keep everything inside just because you don't have people to confide in. The trinity is always with you.

The next step is to put your doubts on hold.

Chapter 4

Suspend Your Doubt

(STEP 3)

"[16] In addition to all this, take up the shield of faith, with which you can extinguish all the flaming arrows of the evil one."

Hang your doubts out to dry. Something will happen during this process that will tempt you to doubt God. This is the time to take a good look at those doubts and shoot them down, hopefully once and for all. If you are having doubts it's because you doubt God will do this for you. Ask yourself, *Why wouldn't He?*

If your answer has something to do with your past or present mistakes, your doubt may be stemming from feelings of unworthiness. Another reason I've encountered doubt is because I was comparing my situation to other people's problems. Comparisons and unworthiness are two faith-barriers that can be knocked down by the word of God.

Dealing With Feelings of Unworthiness- For the children being not yet born, neither having done any good or evil, that the purpose of God according to election might stand, not of works, but of him that calleth; (Romans 9:11)

My greatest barrier to doubt-free living was feeling unworthy. I'd made so many mistakes in my life that I didn't believe I deserved God's help. It's taken years to get over this false belief. Still today my tendency is to wonder if I've been *good enough* to receive what I've asked for.

I believe this partly comes from our childhood conditioning-like not receiving a gift because we'd been more naughty than nice. Or you could only receive something valuable when our behavior was considered good. And sometimes as punishment things were withheld when we were not "good".

When my car broke down or I got sick, I immediately wondered what I'd done wrong. I felt *God must be punishing me.* The truth is adversity comes for different reason.

At times they are results of our own bad judgment; decisions we made based on limited information. Own it. Take responsibility for it and ask God to help you fix it. Other times, challenges are caused by what I call the *Job factor* (Job 1:6). Job was minding his own business, living happily and serving God when BAM! Everything in his life started falling apart.

God is not like man. His gifts do not come with strings attached. Yes there are consequences for doing wrong, but God is not withholding good from us because of our mistakes. **We separate ourselves** from His goodness when we sin. It makes us feel unworthy and unloved. Even then there is forgiveness available to us. Sin is designed to drive a wedge.

The good news is we can remove that wedge anytime. We are worthy and loved because Christ redeemed us, not because of our good behavior. Don't allow feelings of unworthiness to keep you from receiving what God wants you to have-life and more abundantly (John 10:10)

God is not punishing you and you are worthy. So don't give up praying and believing.

Overcoming Negative Comparisons - For God shows no partiality." (Romans 2:11)

One of the ways, I overcome doubt is by refusing to compare my situation to anyone else's. When we compare our journey to others we may (1) limit our expectations to the blessings we see in our neighbor's life (2) Feel like a failure (3) become frustrated and give up (4) open our hearts to envy and jealousy.

It's okay to compare yourself to someone who has achieved a victory that you yourself believe for ONLY if that comparison motivates you. Otherwise, I have found that comparing my journey to my neighbor's is counterproductive.

There's nothing like going through a trial and witnessing the person next to you have breakthrough after breakthrough. You'll start to wonder, *ok God, what about me?*

You have to keep in mind; we are all on our own journey. You never know how long someone had been waiting or what they have endured to get to where they are. Don't compare yourself to them. Instead, use their victory as a motivator. God won't do anything for them that He is not willing to do for you. But, it will be done in His way in His time and custom made for you.

Doubt is a feeling. You have the power to change feelings. It's all about your focus. If you choose to focus on comparisons, limitations, and lack, your doubts will increase.

Give yourself a chance. Even if you are having trouble believing you will get your desired outcome. Resolve to suspend doubt for a period. During my faith fights I usually fast for 21 days as I focus solely on a victorious outcome.

Even after you've prayed, confessed, journaled, and sought advice and support, the enemy still tries to persuade you that your efforts are futile. This persuasion may come in the form of a setback.

When I was faith-fighting the foreclosure, I was actually denied three times. Each time I refused to give up. I went back to step one. I prayed again, *"Lord I was denied. I don't believe this denial is from you. Show me another way to approach this."*

Later that evening I found a website for people facing foreclosure actions. It was actually a forum and hundreds of people just like me were in similar distress. I read through all of the information and one particular suggestion that I believe I was led to. I tried it and that was the beginning of my victory.

God will show you a way if you trust Him and choose not to doubt. As difficult as it may be, and He understands the difficulty of temptation. But He also knows He has placed within you a victorious Spirit that can overcome it.

"There hath no temptation taken you but such as is common to man: but God is faithful, who will not suffer you to be tempted above that ye are able; but will with the temptation also make a way to escape, that ye may be able to bear it." (1 Corinthians 10:13)

I recall these words of a song from my childhood, *"God said it. I believe it and that settles it."* You have to settle in your mind that God has your back. If you don't, everything around you will persuade you to doubt.

About Face!

We've spent several pages talking about problems, doubts, and fears. You've quarantined them; prayed about them; and counseled with your tribe. That's awesome. Now it's time to leave the problem and head in the opposite direction.

It's time to do an about-face. It's time to pivot. Just like a soldier, I want you to make a mental 180 degree turn toward the opposite direction. You're going to do an about-face in your:

- Attitude- turn from negative to positive; from doubt to faith
- Behavior- turn from moping to standing tall; from head down to head held high.
- Perspective- turn from *this is horrible* to *this is working in my favor*

There's a simple thing that I do sometimes that makes me laugh. I want you to try it too. Anytime you have a thought contrary to a victorious thought, I want you to say to yourself, ***about-face***! This is your cue to make a mental turnaround. I see myself in my mind's eye standing at attention and quickly pivoting 180 degrees from my problem toward my promise.

Try it. Have fun with it. See how many times per day you are mentally doing an about-face. Whether you use the exercise above or not, the important thing is that you get into the habit of casting down contrary thoughts immediately, before they turn to doubt.

Now that you've changed directions and you're no longer focused on the problem, you're ready to fully release the outcome to God.

Chapter 5

Make Peace with the Outcome

(STEP 4)

REST. Settle in your mind that God's way is the only way for you. Have the *Hebrew Boys Mindset.* "If we are thrown into the blazing furnace, the God we serve is able to deliver us from it, and he will deliver us from Your Majesty's hand. (Daniel 3:17)

You absolutely must have a *faith mindset* to believe the way they did. Exercise your faith in a way that says, "Yes, my soul, find rest in God; my hope comes from him." (Psalm 62:5)

God doesn't want us to worry about the how or when. Our focus is on maintaining a faith mindset that ushers in the manifestation of deliverance. Surrender the circumstance to God and rest in the knowledge that things are happening behind the heavens that will change things for the better in the physical. I like the seed analogy.

Farmers can't see what's happening with a seed beneath the soil. Similarly, we don't know what God is doing in the Spirit realm. But something IS happening. Take comfort in knowing that the Word you confess, like a seed, knows how to produce all on its own. We just have to create the right conditions for it to thrive. Pray, Meditate day and night; believe; and wait. That's what God wants us to do.

Making Peace with the Outcome

Psalm 71:15-16 I will declare your righteousness and your salvation every day, though I do not fully understand what the outcome will be. Lord God, I will come in the power of your mighty acts, remembering your righteousness—yours alone.

Losing a loved one is one of the most difficult experiences you can have. For me it is *the* most difficult. I've struggled in the past to make peace with the deaths of people most dear to me: mother, aunt, and grandparents to name a few. In some of those cases, I prayed for healing, but they still died. I didn't understand why and honestly I blamed God. The truth is, we don't know all of the reasons why and we will never understand everything in this life.

For many months I closed my heart to God after my mom died suddenly. It didn't make sense. She was in church sun up to sun down. She was faithful in serving. I'm ashamed to admit that I questioned God, *why her? Why not some evil person?* I know that sounds terrible, but I didn't understand. It didn't make sense. I felt powerless; unsure of my own faith; and angry.

That's what happens when we decide that we know best what the outcome should be. We set ourselves up for despair and hopelessness. It's one thing to believe and have faith, but it's quite another to believe that we know more than God. Finding peace with the outcome, even though you can't make sense of it, frees you. It gives you your power back. You live to pray another day with power and conviction.

I also prayed for my marriage to be reconciled, however, it ended in divorce. Now in hindsight, I realize that God gave my ex free will. While, I could have interceded in prayer, I still could not force my will onto him. God would not do that. My faith cannot be used to encroach on someone else's free will. I can intercede, but I cannot control. I also learned that during my oldest son's rebellious years. I interceded for him and praise God he turned back toward God.

Concerning my marriage, I had to admit, I was doing everything counter to what I was praying for. I spoke and thought negatively about my marriage. I was reliving all of the negative. I blamed and totally ignored my faults. Looking back, I sabotaged my own prayers. I didn't have a faith mindset at all.

I've said all of this to say. There are so many moving parts other than your own desire. Don't be so married to a specific outcome that you don't allow God to work the situation out in a way that will be better for you in the long run.

When I was waiting for the mortgage company to give me a decision, on my loan modification, I made in my mind, this is my third attempt and I will still serve God no matter what the outcome. I took on the faith of the Hebrew boys, "*We know our God is well able to deliver us, but if He does not, we still will not bow.*" I had a faith mindset and it prevailed.

I knew my God could change the decision of the mortgage company, but if they denied me, I would still serve God. I would still believe that my latter days would be greater; that my God would never forsake me. Sometimes a delay just means wait and other times it may be a sign to take another route. Whatever you do, don't get discouraged.

There are always laws working that God put in place from the beginning, like sowing and reaping. In the case of my divorce, I accepted responsibility and made peace with myself for any role I may have played and more importantly I made peace with the outcome.

Remember in 2 Samuel 12, when David's son died? He prayed, fasted, and lay before God, but still his son died. He knew that his prayer was contrary to what God had judged, but still he prayed. Though the loss of his son tore him apart, he understood the consequences of his own actions.

In Psalm 51: 1-4, David wrote:

[1]. Have mercy upon me, O God, according to thy lovingkindness: according unto the multitude of thy tender mercies blot out my transgressions.

[2] Wash me thoroughly from mine iniquity, and cleanse me from my sin.

[3] For I acknowledge my transgressions: and my sin is ever before me.

[4] Against thee, thee only, have I sinned, and done this evil in thy sight: that thou mightest be justified when thou speakest, and be clear when thou judgest.

You see while God loves us dearly, there are still consequences for actions we take outside His will. By the grace of God we sometimes escape some of those consequences, but not all consequences can be avoided.

It's important that we learn by the principles in David's example. Acknowledge our wrong; take responsibility; receive forgiveness; and move on-let go of the outcome.

The last thing you want to do is focus on what you've done wrong and all the consequences you deserve. We have something David did not have; the resurrection of Jesus Christ. Thank God for Jesus and receive Mercy and Grace of the Gospel.

Even without the resurrection, David knew that wallowing in condemnation and guilt showed a faithless attitude. He desired to be right with God and He quickly prayed for restoration and asked God to "unseal his lips, that he may praise Him."

David had a faith mindset.

Chapter 6

Demonstrate Your Faith

(STEP 5)

Faith is an action word. Find a way to show that you believe in a positive outcome will truly bless you while you wait. Don't put your head in the sand and just allow things around you to fall apart. Do something constructive. I chose decorating. It will help distract you and help keep you in a positive state of mind.

Find a Project You Enjoy

When I finally pulled myself out of a depressed state about my mortgage situation, I realized that I'd been wallowing in doubt and self-pity far from the faith mindset that I needed. I talked to God and asked for forgiveness for doubting Him. I forgave myself for the role I played in helping to create the financial mess I was in. I stopped beating myself up over not saving; not planning; and so on.

I decided to demonstrate my faith by redecorating my dining room. By doing so, I was showing that I had not given up on remaining in possession of my home. I was investing in it, because it was mine. I started by painting.

Over the course of a few months, I totally changed the look and feel of the dining area. It felt good to complete a project and have such beautiful results. I imagined having family gatherings and birthday parties in my beautiful new space.

Another thing I did was spruce up the yard. I pulled weeds, fertilized the soil and planted grass seed.

Another instance, when I believed for healing, I demonstrated my faith by starting a workout program. I also prayed regularly for people on the "sick and shut-in" list at church. You can do volunteer work to support a cause that is close to your heart.

Your demonstration shows that you believe God's power is real. And even though you are still waiting, you have **complete faith—you know that you know**--without a shadow of a doubt, your victory is on the way.

Sowing Seeds

I sow cash donations quite often. But sewing is more than money. A few years ago, when I was in faith to become a published author, I sowed into several author's ministries by donating and purchasing the books.

I believe in the principle of sowing and reaping. Too often we say, "You reap what you sow" in a negative way, but if you think about it, that's good news! A seed is anything that you give of yourself including but not limited to:

- Volunteer Time
- Dollars or other forms of currency
- Donations of your knowledge, skills, and abilities
- Gifts
- Spiritual encouragement
- Products and services from your business

Again, a seed is not always money. Ask God for wisdom about sowing as it pertains to your personal circumstance. What you give comes back to you. As the song goes, *you can't beat God giving no matter how you try*. God does not need your seed. He needs you to develop a heart of giving so that the principle of sowing and reaping can bless your life.

Resolve To Operate on a Spiritual Level

We absolutely have to get into the habit of living by spiritual laws. The world tells us that life happens to us and we should *just roll with the punches*. That's not how believers live. Life does not happen to us. We happen to life. We operate in faith-mode. We believe in the spirit of God that works in us to accomplish great and mighty things. As such, we deliberately take action by faith. In scripture after scripture, God says, *if you do this, then this will happen*. For example:

- If you seek, you will find. (Matthew 7:7)
- If you give, you will receive. (Luke 6:38)
- If you sow, you will reap. (Galatians 6:7)
- If you pray, I will hear you. (Job 22:27)
- If you believe, you shall receive. (Mark 11:24)

So if you have a need, there is a way of obtaining that need. If you have a desire that is aligned with the will of God, there is a way of achieving that desire. Regardless of what naysayers tell you; what the medical exam shows; or what you've experienced in the past, the spiritual laws of our Lord are the authority.

When you choose to walk, talk, and think in line with spiritual laws, you are walking in faith. You are operating in your God-given authority and dominion. Take hold of God's promises. Demonstrate your faith in your conversation; attitude; and behaviors. The more you do, the more it will become second nature to walk by faith, not by sight.

Chapter 7

Wait and Stand Firm

(STEP 6)

"Therefore put on the full armor of God, so that when the day of evil comes, you may be able to stand your ground, and after you have done everything, to stand."

Waiting is hard. It's especially difficult when you are challenged in the area of patience like I am.

No matter what it is, as I get older, I notice I want things to happen faster. Naturally, because I feel this way, I get the opposite result. Sowing impatience only invites more opportunity for me to be tested in the area of patience. Waiting in grocery store lines is a prime example.

Invariably, something will happen with the person in front of me. Either they will need a price check for an item that takes forever, or they have some other issue that requires a manager to be paged.

Years ago, I'd roll my eyes; sigh really hard; and suck my teeth. Now when I wait in line, I just take a deep breath and choose to wait with a good attitude. Hey I'm getting better. No huffing and puffing like a whiney toddler any more. I had to develop patience.

It's a daily thing for me. And I can honestly say I'm not tested nearly as much in this area lately.

Keep Calm and Wait with Patience

For me, the waiting is the hardest part. David expressed in Psalm 40, the blessing in waiting patiently on Lord:

"I waited patiently for the Lord to help me, and he turned to me and heard my cry. He lifted me out of the pit of despair, out of the mud and the mire. He set my feet on solid ground and steadied me as I walked along. He has given me a new song to sing, a hymn of praise to our God. Many will see what He has done and be amazed. They will put their trust in the Lord." (Psalm 40:1-3)

Though David had to go through a waiting period, it's evident in the Psalm, that he didn't feel abandoned or alone. He recognized God's presence. God is with you, even in the dark days.

The best advice I can give in a tense faith fight is *calm down*. Getting worked up and emotionally overwhelmed will not serve you. Worry will completely derail you. Trust me, I know, sometimes life sucks. I'll admit that. We can't control what happens all the time, but it's the mindset that will get you through it.

No matter how much the children of Israel grumbled and complained God was still with them. He is still with you too. He knows that you are frustrated and at your wits end. Why do you think He has me writing this message (smile)?

"Teaching them to observe all things whatsoever I have commanded you: and, lo, I am with you always, even unto the end of the world. Amen." (Matthew 28:20)

The Father wants you to know that you are going to reach your destination, but waiting is part of the process. How long you wait depends on you and the details of your circumstances. Doubt, fear, grumbling and complaining are all signs of *failing faith* and make waiting that much more difficult. In some cases, grumbling will even prolong the breakthrough.

Hebrews 6:11, 12, "We want each of you to show the same diligence to the very end, so that your hope may be fully assured. (12) Then you will not be sluggish, but will imitate those who through faith and patience inherit what has been promised.

You've prayed. You know that God has heard you. You believe His word is true. I want you to remember two things (1) You're not alone and (2) The Promised Land does exist.

Where Is My Promised Land?

The Children of Israel are prime examples of what not to do while you're waiting on your promise. Maybe you feel like your circling the wilderness right now. Let's see if we can learn a few lessons from the children of Israel when it comes to waiting and being patient.

They refused to change their mindset. They grumbled, complained and whined just as they did when they were slaves. They didn't have a faith mindset.

- God provided provision but they were *never satisfied*.
- God rescued them but they *didn't appreciate* the miraculous rescue.
- They didn't reach the Promised Land right away so they *doubted*.
- They *complained.*

They grumbled. That was a huge contributor to the delay of their entrance into the land God promised them.

They turned from God. While you wait, know that your blessing is on the way. Don't guess it's on the way, or wonder if it's on the way…you have to KNOW it. Try not to be concerned with the *hows:*

- How long is going to take?
- How is it even possible?

- How many times have I tried and failed?
- How many people actually achieve this?

Make Peace with God's Timing

Solomon said, "There is a time for everything, and a season for every activity under the heavens:" (Ecclesiastes 3:1)

You will only have peace during the faith process when you accept the fact that God's timing is perfect, regardless of how it looks to you in the moment. Failure to accept God's timing could result in increased doubt; self-sabotage; and making impulsive decision.

When Abraham and Sarah doubted God's promise for a son, they took matters into their own hands. Sarah gave her handmaid to her husband Abraham and yes, a son was born, but this is not what God had planned. People were hurt. Hearts were broken. They failed to wait on God and caused confusion. God is not the author of confusion.

In God's timing Isaac was born just has He promised. Had Abraham and Sarah waited, the confusion and pain would have been avoided.

God adores you profoundly. He is so thrilled to bless you. Blessings are received by faith. Breakthroughs are received by faith.

"Wait for the LORD; Be strong and let your heart take courage; Yes, wait for the LORD." (Psalm 27:14)

Trusting in God's timing can be difficult when you can't see how, but remember if God promised it, he will deliver it. Leave the *how* and *when* to Him. Try to find pleasure in knowing somehow you will receive the right outcome in the right season.

> "14 Stand firm then, with the belt of truth buckled around your waist, with the breastplate of righteousness in place, 15 and with your feet fitted with the readiness that comes from the gospel of peace."

Find peace in the waiting phase. Know that it is just that a phase. It is temporary. Anticipate the blessing, because it is on the way. Wait for it.

Chapter 8

Rehearse Your Celebration

(STEP 7)

Psalm 71:15-16 I will declare your righteousness and your salvation every day, though I do not fully understand what the outcome will be. Lord God, I will come in the power of your mighty acts, remembering your righteousness—yours alone.

Have Joyful Anticipation

You don't need to have the outcome in order to feel joyful. Anticipation is defined as, "prospect, outlook, **anticipation**, foretaste mean an advance realization of something to come,"

It's okay to go ahead and get excited about what has already taken place in the spirit realm. When you prayed, God answered and it is done. Get that in your spirit. It's already done for you in the heavens.

You have faith right now. It's your ***now faith*** that is the substance of your victory! Not the faith you will have after you receive what you prayed for, but the faith you have right now that it's already done. Your faith is your evidence. Hold to that faith joyfully as you anticipate it materializing before your eyes.

God has given you an advance realization of the good things to come. He has given you a measure of faith. Your faith is a sneak peak of your breakthrough. That's powerful. Really meditate on that for a minute. The measure of faith God gave you, is the answer to your prayer. If you have faith, you already have your breakthrough. Glory to God. That's a reason to shout *Victory!*

Rehearse Your Victory

How are you going to react when everything works out in your favor? What are you going to do? Say? How are you going to feel? That's what I want you to rehearse.

When I finally received the great news that my mortgage modification had been approved after three denials, I was relieves, overjoyed, happy, and downright giddy.

I danced around my living room. I called one of my tribe members and testified. I shouted, "Thank you Jesus!" I even shed a tear.

Think of your own reaction. Rehearse your victory speech. What does your testimony sound like? What are you going to Post, Snap, Tweet, or Chat about? Are you going to dance?

Whatever you are going to do, go ahead and do it now. Give God the glory now. Usher in the presence of God through your praise and watch how heaven and earth move in response to your faithful praise.

I know some of you may be in a difficult place. If you can't bring yourself to dance, then just raise your hands to heave and say, *Thank you Jesus.* Ask the Holy Spirit to guide you into a place of peace and open your heart to receive the healing love of God.

Maintain a Joyfully Eager Attitude As Much As Possible

Think of your breakthrough as a seven-figure, tax-free check on its way to your address paid to the order of you—imagine that feeling of excited expectation. It's arriving any day now and the only thing between you and that blessing is the time it takes for it to travel from its destination to you.

Or imagine someone you love dearly, but haven't seen in many years, is coming to visit and will be arriving any minute. What does that feel like? Can you hardly contain yourself?

Practice those feelings. That's how God wants you to feel about what's in store for you. Stand on your faith. Walk it out through demonstration; conversations; and your imagination.

If it gets hard and you feel like you want to quit, pray. Ask the Holy Spirit for guidance. He's your teacher and your guide. Ask for help and then pick yourself up and keep going.

Little by little you will become stronger. Your joy will return. The frown lines will lessen and you will smile again.

Testify of God's Goodness

Let me encourage you to share your testimony. I don't mean tell the world every detail of your person life; but do share the Good news about what God is doing or has done in your life.

The woman at the well told everyone about the man who cured her thirst. The lame mane testified of Jesus' healing power. I'm testifying before you today. I was once depressed and emotionally drained. Now I'm strengthened and at peace.

Share your story. Don't let your victory be locked away, but let it be a light that shines bright for the lost and hurting. I read this quote the other day, "Your story is the key that can unlock someone else's prison." (Unknown).

It is true that God will turn your test into a testimony. You may not feel like you have one yet and that's okay. The more you walk by faith, the more miracles and favor you will experience.

Daniel 4:2 "I want you all to know about the miraculous signs and wonders the Most High God has performed for me.

There's going to come a time when you will have an opportunity to share the testimony that you rehearsed and it will change someone's life.

Chapter 9

Conclusion

(Review & Wrap Up)

Now Faith is

Faith works. Faith is the immediate answer to your prayer. It is the evidence that your victory is guaranteed. Faith *is*. We are the righteousness of God in Christ. God has given us all a measure of faith. We must believe that our faith is the evidence of every Godly desire we have. Only by faith can we obtain God's promises.

It is your faith that will give you the strength to fight on when every natural instinct you have says, *quit,* or *give up.* It is your faith that will unlock spiritual power and engage spiritual laws.

Let's review the *Faith Strategy steps again*:

1. Quarantine the Issue: Don't expose it yet.
2. Go Before The Throne of Grace: Talk to God first.
3. Assemble The Tribe: Seek Godly advice.
4. Suspend Your Doubts: It's not by your strength, but by God's power.
5. Surrender It To God: Let it go and leave it to God.

6. Demonstrate Your Faith: Walk it out in your attitude, actions, and communication.
7. Wait and Know: Divine timing is part of the process. Wait with joyful anticipation.
8. Rehearse Your Celebration: Imagine yourself celebrating and testifying.

At the end of the book, I've listed several statements to consider daily. It's entitled the **Faith Strategy Accountability Checklist** and is intended to remind you of all the spiritually uplifting tools and resources you have at your disposal every minute of the day. Here are the statements (in question form):

1. Have you prayed an honest, fruitful prayer today?
2. Did you pray for someone else today?
3. Did you do a kind deed today? (includes praying, interceding for someone else)
4. Did you read and or meditate on at least one scripture pertaining to your issue?
5. Were you able to do at least two things that made you happy/smile/laugh?
6. Did you write down or reflect on three things that you are grateful for?
7. Have you reflected on at least one victory God has given you in the past?
8. Did you declare, in *Jesus name, I am victorious* today?
9. How did you demonstrate your faith today?

(1) Fruitful prayers are open and honest with God about fears, doubts, and desires. Prayers open with thanksgiving and end with appreciation and praise. **(2)** By praying for someone else you are activating the principles of loving your neighbor and of sowing and reaping.

When you pray for others, you love your neighbor (the great commandment) and you open the door for others to pray and intercede for results in your situation. **(3)** The same is true with doing a kind deed. Scripture says God will do the same for you. (Ephesians 6:8).

(4) Meditate on the word of God and expect success. "This Book of the Law shall not depart from your mouth, but you shall meditate on it day and night, so that you may be careful to do according to all that is written in it. For then you will make your way prosperous, and then you will have good success." (Joshua 1:8)

(5) Do at least two things that made you happy/smile/laugh "A merry heart doeth good *like* a medicine: but a broken spirit drieth the bones." (Proverbs 17:22)

(6) Write down or reflect on three things that you are grateful for.

- "Give thanks in all circumstances; for this is God's will for you in Christ Jesus" (1 Thessalonians 5:18).
- "Thanks be to God, who delivers me through Jesus Christ our Lord!" (Romans 7:25).
- "Do not be anxious about anything, but in every situation, by prayer and petition, with thanksgiving, present your requests to God" (Philippians 4:6).

(7) Reflect on at least one victory God has given you in the past.

(8) Declare, in *Jesus name, I am victorious* today!

(9) Demonstrate your faith. "[17] Thus also faith by itself, if it does not have works, is dead." (James 2:14:17)

Doing these things each day will reinforce a faith mindset and keep you focused on victory and ensure that your faith endures. "But I have prayed for thee, that thy faith fail not: and when thou art converted, strengthen thy brethren. (Luke 22:32)

In time they will come easily and you will do without thinking about it. Every time you do, you're operating from a *faith mindset* and practicing your own *Faith Strategy*.

I promised

In the Introduction, I promised to share my personal *Faith Strategy* in a simple, down-to-earth, relatable, and to-the-point—way. I hope that I kept that promise. As I said some day it may change, but to date this modality works for me. God has shown up in some really great ways and I'm so thankful.

I hope that you will be inspired to take identify your own. If there are areas you feel need work, don't feel bad or ashamed, just work on them. We are all a work in progress. We learn. We do and we grow.

God bless you in your faith walk. I pray that your faith grows and your life is filled with favor and blessings beyond what you ever believed possible in the past. Remember if you have faith, you already have the victory. "**Now faith is** the substance of things hoped for, the evidence of things not seen." (Hebrews 11:1)

END

Faith Strategy Accountability Checklist

- ○ I've thanked God today that I already have what I prayed for.
- ○ I prayed for someone else today.
- ○ I sowed a kind deed today (includes praying, interceding for someone else)
- ○ I read and meditated on at least one scripture pertaining to my situation.
- ○ I was able to do at least two things that made me happy/smile/laugh.
- ○ I wrote/reflected on three things that I am grateful for.
- ○ I reflected on at least one victory God has given me in the past.
- ○ I listened to my favorite song today.
- ○ I made a faith declaration today.
- ○ I imagined, in detail, how it would feel to testify about my victory.
- ○ I demonstrated my faith today.

Faith Strategy Action Steps

- #1 Quarantine The Issue
- #2 Go Before The Throne of Grace
- #3 Assemble The Tribe
- #4 Suspend Your Doubts
- #5 Surrender It To God
- #6 Demonstrate Your Faith
- #7 Wait and Know
- #8 Rehearse Your Celebration

If you enjoyed this title, please leave a comment on Amazon. I appreciate this time with you. God bless!

Did you know this book has a study guide?

Read my 21 day fast journal, 21 Days of Fasting and Prayer: My Personal Daniel Fast Journal

Join my mailing list for notification of the next Book in this series: *The Grace to Go Through: By God's Grace You Will Make It*

****

Bestselling Titles

Deliver Me From Negative Self Talk A Guide To Speaking Faith-filled Words

How God Sees Your Struggles: Encouraging Yourself, Finding Strength & Developing A Spiritual Perspective

Deliver Me From Negative Emotions: Controlling Negative Emotions and Finding Peace In The Storm

Want Free E-Books?

From time to time Lynn gives away free copies of her new releases. But some of these promotions are temporary. If you'd like to know when Lynn's books are available for FREE, just visit the blog LynnRDavis.com and register your email today.

****

ABOUT THE AUTHOR

Bestselling Indie and Hybrid Author, Lynn R. Davis writes non-denominational inspirational, spiritual growth, and personal development nonfiction books.

She enjoys uplifting readers and encouraging them to push past painful disappointments and onward to breakthrough and deliverance. Her negative self-talk books continue to make a huge impact in the lives of readers around the world.

Sharing God's word is her passion. She is the mother of two boys; a grandmother of a beautiful little girl; and the doting Aunt of 15 nieces and nephews.

70189982R00042

Made in the USA
San Bernardino, CA
26 February 2018